Dance

Salsa

By Trudy Becker

level 2
little blue readers

www.littlebluehousebooks.com

Little Blue House is distributed by North Star Editions:
sales@northstareditions.com | 888-417-0195

Produced for Little Blue House by Red Line Editorial.

Photographs ©: iStockphoto, cover, 4, 7, 10, 13, 15, 19, 21, 24 (top left), 24 (bottom left), 24 (bottom right); Shutterstock Images, 9, 16, 23, 24 (top right)

Library of Congress Control Number: 2022919969

ISBN
978-1-64619-831-3 (hardcover)
978-1-64619-860-3 (paperback)
978-1-64619-915-0 (ebook pdf)
978-1-64619-889-4 (hosted ebook)

Printed in the United States of America
Mankato, MN
082023

About the Author

Trudy Becker lives in Minneapolis, Minnesota. She likes exploring new places and loves anything involving books.

Table of Contents

Move to the Music **5**

What Is Salsa? **11**

Learning How **17**

Glossary **24**

Index **24**

Move to the Music

Salsa dancers swirl
around the stage.
They move to the rhythm
of the music.

A pair dances together.
One dancer holds, and
the other twirls.
They work as a team.

pair

Another pair shifts
their weight.
They stay together and hit
every beat.
They are dancing salsa.

What Is Salsa?

Salsa is a type of Latin dance. It started in Cuba and New York. Puerto Rican and Caribbean artists helped make it.

In salsa, dancers move their weight from foot to foot.

Their steps have a pattern.

Salsa usually happens in pairs.

One partner leads the motions, and the other partner follows.

Learning How

Salsa dancers practice with their partners. They must work together. Then they perform or compete.

Salsa outfits are colorful.
Sometimes dancers wear fancy skirts.
The skirts show their fast moves and spins.

skirt

Salsa dancers wear hard shoes or high heels. The shoes help them balance and turn.

high heel

Dancers stretch before every show.
They make sure their partners are ready.
It is time to salsa dance!

Glossary

high heels

practice

pair

skirt

Index

L

Latin dance, 11

O

outfits, 18

P

practice, 17

R

rhythm, 5